To my YesKid: _____

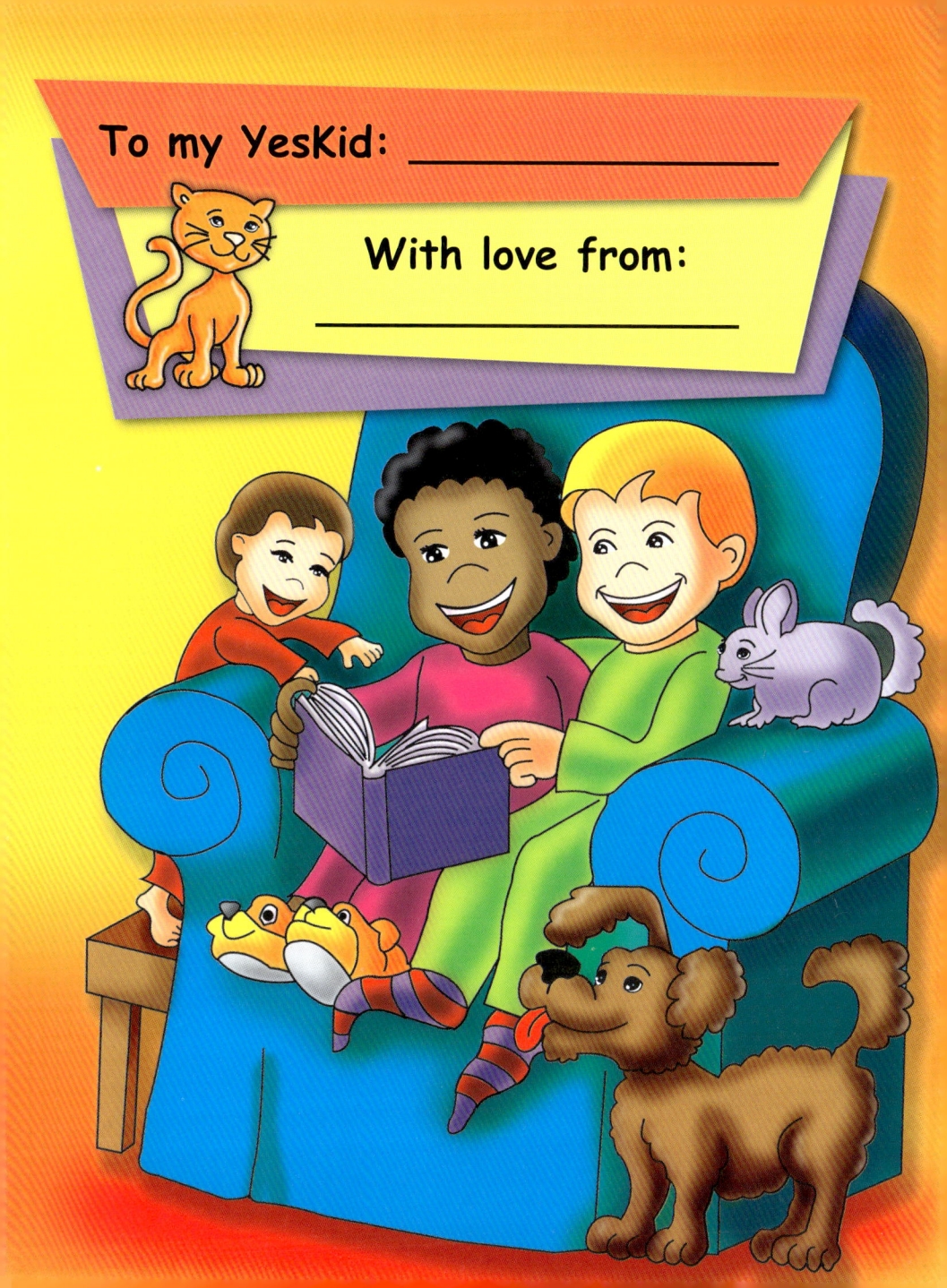

With love from:
_____

The YesKids Bible
Stories & Prayers

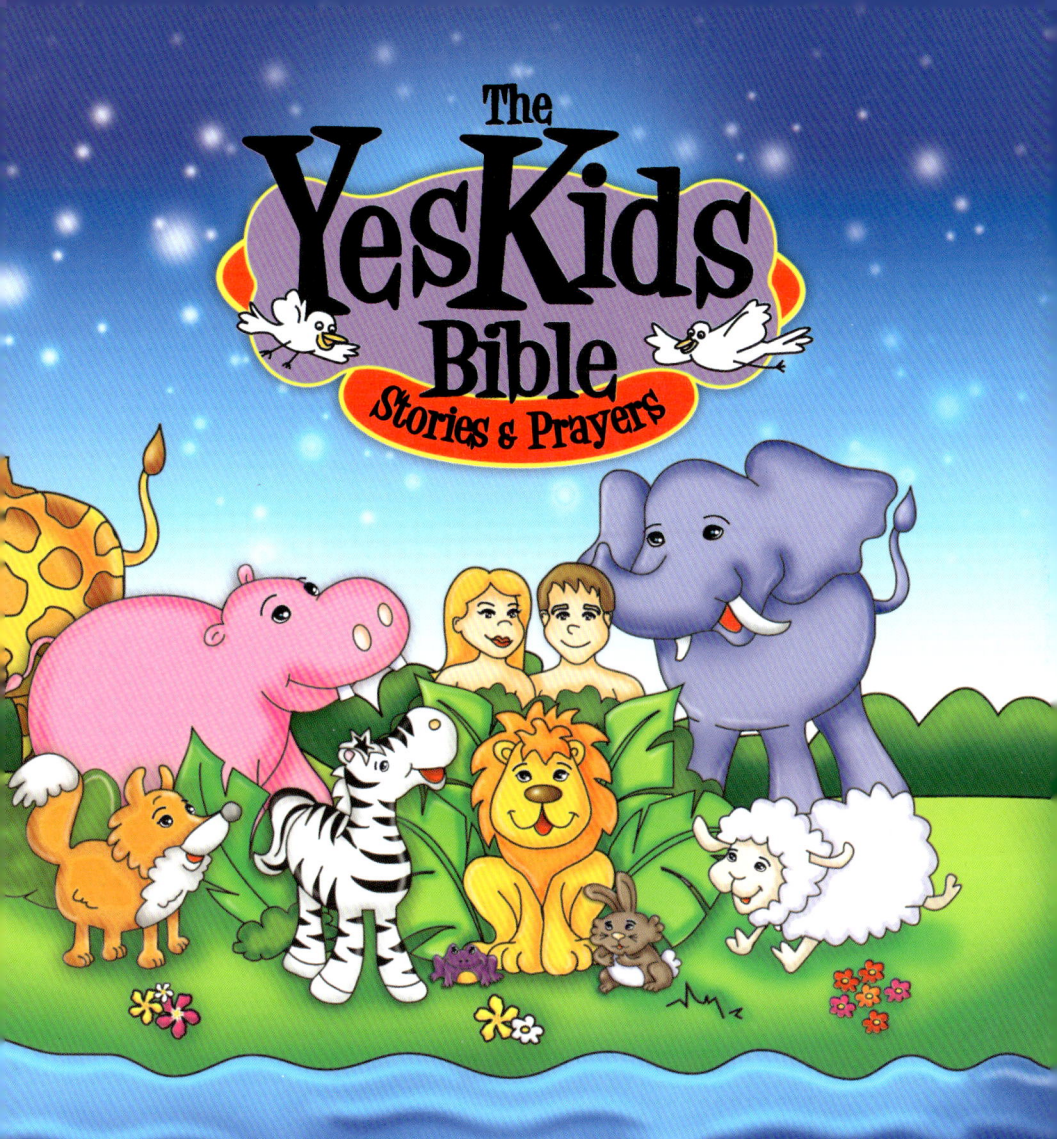

cmp
christian media publishing **kids**
pointing children in the **right direction**

Note to parents

We hope you will enjoy reading these stories to your child. There are several ways you can enjoy this Bible together:
- You can read the stories first and then play the guessing game with your child.
- Once your child is familiar with the stories you can go through the book playing the guessing game.

The Bible stories have been retold in words that small children can easily understand, while still remaining faithful to the message of Scripture. Throughout, our aim has been to help children develop a strong and loving relationship with God. The words and pictures further emphasise Biblical values. You can use the pictures to stimulate discussions about God and faith.

At the end of each story you will find a prayer to pray and a value or message to share with your child. Look out for the animal friends who appear in the Bible stories. One of them will help the child to remember the message or value of the story. The other one provides the key to the guessing game which accompanies each story.

This book of Bible stories is so much more than a story book. Use it to teach children the joy and meaning of being a Christian, and what Jesus can mean in their lives.

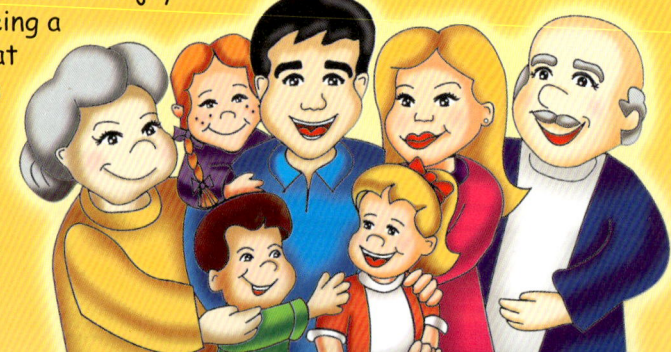

Contents

1. My God is so great! — 8
2. Always listen to God — 12
3. Nothing is impossible with God — 16
4. God makes a donkey talk! — 20
5. God hears when you pray — 24
6. Speak Lord, I'm listening — 28
7. Wise King Solomon — 32
8. God provides food and water — 36
9. God is much stronger than Baal — 40
10. Nehemiah helps to make Jerusalem beautiful again — 44
11. With God's help — 48
12. Daniel in the Lion's Den — 52
13. Jonah disobeys God — 56
14. Jesus is born — 60
15. Jesus visits the temple — 64
16. Five loaves and two fish — 68
17. There is no one like Jesus — 72
18. A father opens his arms — 76
19. The ten girls — 80
20. Bad Zacchaeus becomes Good Zacchaeus — 84
21. Here comes king Jesus — 88
22. Jesus loves his friends — 92
23. The cross — 96
24. Jesus has risen from the dead! — 100
25. Jesus returns home — 104

Guidelines for Parents — 108

1. My God is so great!
(Genesis 1 & 2)

God made our beautiful world.
First he made the light. He made the sun to shine in the day, and the moon and stars to shine at night. He also made the sea and the land. Then he made the plants and trees. There were flowers, fruit trees and vegetables everywhere.

Our great God also made
other things for this wonderful world,
like the fish that swim and
the birds that sing so sweetly.
He made the wild animals,
tame animals, insects and bugs.
Everything comes from God.

Then God did something very special ... He made the first people. The man was called Adam and the woman was called Eve. The Lord loved them very much!

Come, let's pray together:

Lord, you are so great. There is nothing that you can't do. Thank you for making such a beautiful world. Amen.

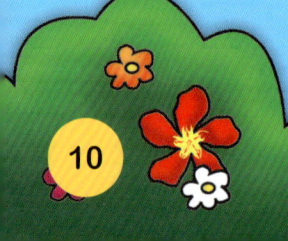

God made all the wonderful things in the world.

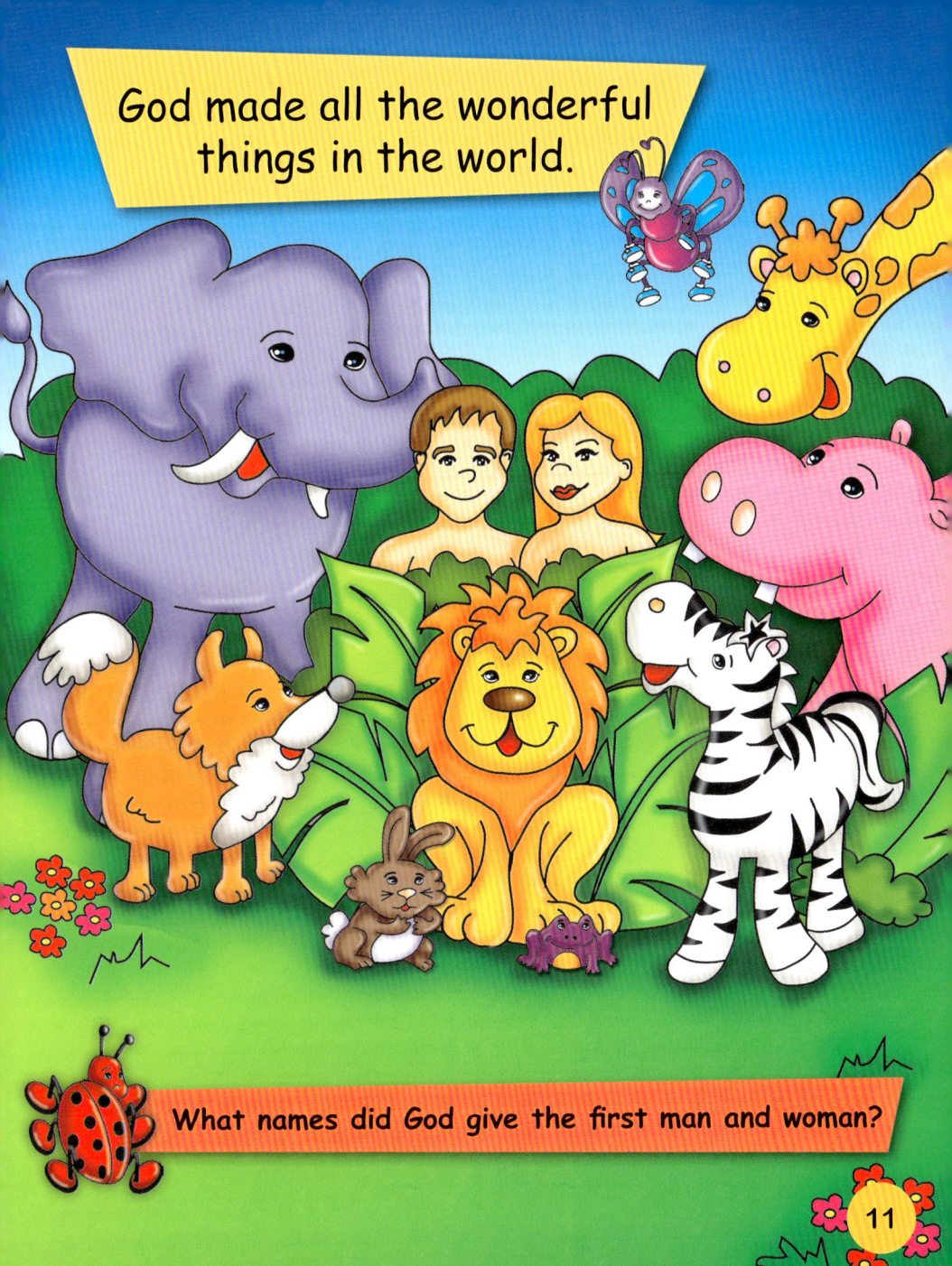

What names did God give the first man and woman?

11

2. Always listen to God!
(Genesis 3)

God put Adam and Eve in a beautiful place called the Garden of Eden.
It was a lovely place to live. God said to them, "You can eat everything you find here. But there is one special tree; you may not eat the fruit growing on this tree. If you do you will surely die."

One day the evil devil disguised himself as a snake. He talked to Eve and told her terrible lies. He said, "You can eat the fruit on this special tree. You will not die, like God says you will."

13

Then Adam and Eve ate some fruit from the tree. God was very sad when he saw that they had disobeyed him. As a result, they had to leave the Garden of Eden.

Bad things happen when we don't listen to God. Luckily for us, Jesus made everything right again when he gave his life for us.

Come, let's pray together:

Dear Father, please help me
to always listen to you.
Amen.

Jesus washed away our sins.
Always listen to God.

Where did Adam and Eve live?

3. Nothing is impossible with God!
(Genesis 12, 13, 15, 17, 18 & 21)

God told Abraham that he had to leave his home for another country. Abraham took his wife Sarah, and his nephew Lot with him.

They were happy for a while, but then Lot's workers and Abraham's workers began to argue. It's always so horrible when people fight. So Abraham told Lot, "We must live in different places. You choose first where you want to live." Lot chose the best land for himself.

17

God had promised Abraham that he would care for him and give him a very big family; but Abraham and Sarah had no children.

They wanted children very much, but they were getting old. Had God forgotten his promise to them?

One day three men came to visit. They told Abraham that Sarah would soon have a baby boy. When Sarah heard this, she laughed. God wanted to know why she was laughing. Had she forgotten that God can do anything?

And a short while later a baby boy was born to Sarah and Abraham. They called him Isaac.

What were Isaac's dad and mom's names?

Come, let's pray together:

Thank you, Lord, that you care for me and that with you nothing is impossible. Amen.

God can do much more than people can! Nothing is impossible with him.

4. God makes a donkey talk!
(Numbers 22)

King Balak offered to pay Balaam a lot of money to say bad things about God's chosen people. But God decided to stop Balaam.

Balaam was riding his donkey on his way to King Balak. Suddenly an angel of the Lord appeared in the road. He was holding a sword.

Only the donkey could see the angel. Balaam could not see him at all.

Three times, the donkey turned off the road to avoid the angel.
Each time Balaam hit the donkey.

Name the man whose donkey spoke to him?

22

Then the Lord opened Balaam's eyes, and suddenly he also saw the angel. The angel said to him, "From now on you will say what God tells you to say." And that is exactly what Balaam did.

Come, let's pray together:

Dear God, help me not to say nasty things about other people. Amen.

Jesus does not like it when we say nasty things about other people.

5. God hears when you pray
(1 Samuel 1)

Elkanah and his wife Hannah lived in a small village. The people of the village teased Hannah because she could not have children. This made her very unhappy.

Hannah prayed in the temple that God would give her a baby. She cried while she prayed.

Eli, the priest, saw her crying and he thought she was drunk. He scolded her. But when she told him her story he realised that she was not drunk. She was just very, very sad.

So Eli said to her, "God will give you a baby." And it happened just as Eli said it would. The baby was born and they called him Samuel.

God was good to Hannah, because after Samuel she had another five children. And nobody ever teased her again.

Come, let's pray together:

Thank you, Jesus, that you always hear my prayers. Amen.

Jesus doesn't like it when we tease other people.

Which lady couldn't have a baby?

6. Speak Lord, I am listening!
(1 Samuel 3)

Early one morning something special happened to Samuel. He was living with Eli in the temple, but Eli was still asleep. A voice called, "Samuel!"
Samuel answered, "I'm coming!"

Quickly he ran to Eli. "You called me. Here I am," he said to the sleepy Eli. Eli shook his head. "I didn't call you," he said. When it happened a second time, Eli realised that it was God who was calling Samuel. So Eli said to Samuel, "The next time someone calls your name, say 'Speak Lord, I'm listening.'"

This is exactly what Samuel did, and the Lord spoke to him.

29

He would remember it until the day he died. From that day on everybody talked about Samuel, who always did what the Lord asked him to do.

Come, let's pray together:

Lord Jesus, help me always listen to the things you say to me in the Bible. Amen.

These days the Lord talks to us through the Bible.

The Lord spoke to............?

7. Wise King Solomon
(1 Kings 3)

One night King Solomon dreamed that God asked him, "What is the one thing you want the most from me?" "Help me to make wise choices," Solomon answered. So God made Solomon the wisest person in the whole world.

One day two women came to see King Solomon. They brought a baby with them. Each of the women said the baby was hers.

One woman's baby had died in the night, so she had stolen the other woman's baby. But which woman was telling the truth? Who was the real mother?

Solomon made a clever plan. "Cut the baby in half." he said. "Then each of you will get half a baby."

Straight away one woman said, "Yes, cut him in half." But the other woman said, "No, please, rather give the baby to her. Just don't kill him."

Solomon immediately knew the second woman was the real mother, because she really cared about the baby. So he gave the baby to her.

Everybody talked about his great wisdom.

Come, let's pray together:

Jesus, help me to bring you joy every day by listening to you. Amen.

Remember to pray every day.

Who was a very wise king?

35

8. God provides food and water
(1 Kings 17)

Elijah was a man who talked to the Israelites about God. But King Ahab and the rest of the Israelites refused to listen to God's message.

So Elijah told King Ahab that it would not rain for a very long time, because he would not serve God. King Ahab decided to have Elijah killed. God told Elijah to hide away in a cave near a stream. There, Elijah had enough water to drink, but he had no food. He grew very hungry. So God sent crows with meat and bread in their beaks.

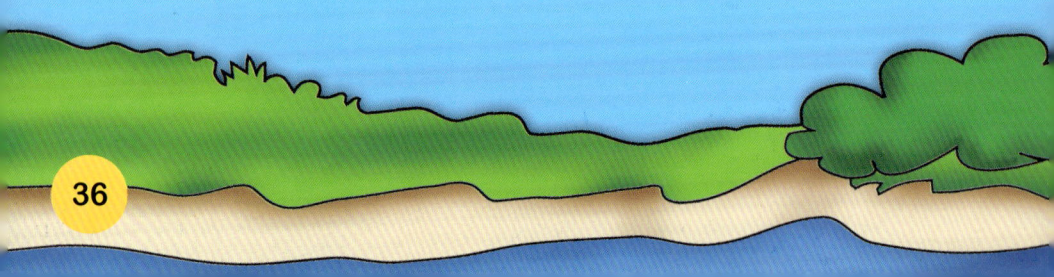

37

They brought food to Elijah twice a day, in the morning and in the evening.

Elijah knew that God would always care for him.

Come, let's pray together:

Dear Father, thank you that you always take care of me. Amen.

Always say thank you to Jesus that you have enough to eat and drink.

Whom did God send the crows to feed?

39

9. God is much stronger than Baal (1 Kings 18)

Elijah went to King Ahab and his fierce wife Jezebel. He said to them, "I am going to prove to you that God is much more powerful than your god Baal. Ask Baal to set this pile of wood on fire. I will ask God the same thing."

Nothing happened, Baal did not set the wood on fire. There was no sign of life from him at all. Then Elijah poured water onto his wood pile and prayed.

41

God set the sopping wet wood alight. Everyone saw that God was greater and more powerful than Baal.

Still Elijah was not finished. "God is going to make it rain now," he said. The sky was clear, except for a small cloud the size of a man's hand.

King Ahab and the rest of the people could not believe their eyes, as they watched the sky turned dark with rain clouds and it began to rain ... and rain ... and rain.

There is no one as powerful as our God.

Come, let's pray together:

Our Father God, thank you that you are so strong and so good to us. Amen.

God is great, and there is nothing that He can't do.

Do you know the names of the king and queen?

10. Nehemiah helps to make Jerusalem beautiful again

(Nehemiah 1 - 7)

Nehemiah was an Israelite. He was the cupbearer in the palace of the Persian king. This was an important job, because he had to taste everything served to the king, to make sure it wasn't poisoned.

Some of the Israelites who had returned to Jerusalem told him how terrible the city was looking. Even the city walls had been destroyed. God wanted Nehemiah to return to Jerusalem to help his people rebuild the city. Nehemiah loved God very much.

He realised he had to ask the Persian king to allow him to return to Jerusalem right away. He was rather scared about what the king would say, so he prayed before speaking to the king. The Lord answered his prayer. Nehemiah returned to Jerusalem. There they rebuilt the city beautifully, and promised to obey God forever.

Come, let's pray together:

Dear Father, help me always to obey you so I can also do wonderful things for you. Amen.

Nothing makes us happier than loving God.

Who rebuilt the walls of Jerusalem?

47

11. With God's help
(Esther 1 - 10)

Esther was a very beautiful woman. She was so beautiful that the king of Persia made her his wife and queen.

One day her uncle Mordecai, came to visit her. He said to her, "All the Jewish people — including you and me — are in serious trouble. That wicked man Haman, wants to kill all of us. He told the king lies about us and now the king has made a law saying that on a particular day all the Jews must be murdered."

Mordecai fell to his knees in front of Esther and said, "Please Esther, help us. Only you can save us."

Esther invited the king and the evil Haman to dinner.

She told the king about Haman's plans to kill her and her people.

The king was very angry with Haman. He made a new law that saved the Jews. The Jews were so happy they all danced in the streets.

Esther was a brave woman who saved her people with God's help.

Come, let's pray together:

Dear God, I help other people because I love you so much. Amen.

God uses ordinary people, like you and me and Esther, to help others.

Name the brave and beautiful young woman?

12. Daniel in the Lion's Den
(Daniel 6)

Daniel was a very important Jew who lived in Persia. Everyone knew how much he loved God. He prayed three times every day. Some people were jealous of him, so they told King Darius to make a new law saying people could only pray to the king, not to God.

Anybody who disobeyed that law would be thrown to the lions. Daniel did not care about the new law. He carried on praying to God as usual: morning, noon and evening.

The jealous people told the king that Daniel was breaking the law.

53

So Daniel was thrown into a den filled with lions. God closed the lions' mouths and Daniel was safe. Then the king knew that Daniel's God was the only true God.

Come, let's pray together:

Jesus, my life
is safe in your hands.
Amen.

God can help you too, just as he helped Daniel in the lion's den.

Who was thrown into the lion's den?

55

13. Jonah disobeys God
   (Jonah 2)

God told Jonah to go to the people of Nineveh and to tell them to stop sinning. He did not want to obey God so Jonah tried to run away from God. He sailed away on a boat. Jonah didn't realise that nobody can run away from God, because he sees everything.

Suddenly a storm blew up around Jonah's boat. Everyone on the boat was afraid. The sailors threw Jonah into the sea. God sent a large fish to save Jonah and it swallowed him up. Inside the fish's tummy Jonah told God that he was sorry he had run away.

The fish spat Jonah out onto the beach. Quickly Jonah went to Nineveh and did what God asked. He told the people to stop doing bad things. They said: "Lord, we are sorry," and God forgave them. This made Jonah angry, because he did not like the people of Nineveh. God said he loves everybody and that is why he forgave them.

Come, let's pray together:

Jesus, help me always to say sorry when I do something wrong. Amen.

Say you're sorry if you have done wrong. Jesus loves everyone, you too.

Who tried to run away from God?

14. Jesus is born
(Luke 1 & 2)

Mary lived in the town of Nazareth. She was engaged to Joseph.
One day she had a visitor.
This wasn't just anybody; it was one of God's archangels, Gabriel, who paid her a visit. He told her that she was going to have a baby, and this baby would be the Son of God. "How can this happen?" Mary asked. "I am not married yet."

Gabriel told her not to worry, because nothing is impossible with God. The baby would be a miracle sent from heaven.

61

Mary answered the angel, "Tell God I am willing to obey. He can do anything he wants with me." The angel left, and her life was never the same again. Mary and Joseph were married later. It was the greatest moment when the special baby from heaven was born in Bethlehem and she held him in her arms. Joseph called the baby Jesus. Yes, this baby Jesus would change the whole world.

Come, let's pray together:

Lord, I worship and praise you because nothing is impossible with you. Amen.

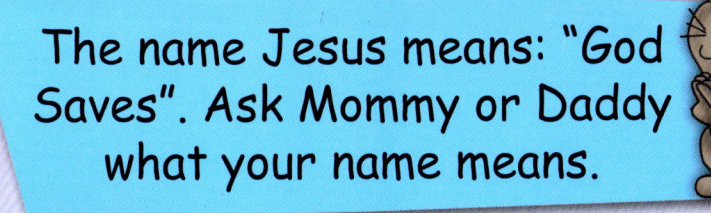

The name Jesus means: "God Saves". Ask Mommy or Daddy what your name means.

Where was Jesus born?

15. Jesus visits the temple
(Luke 2)

Jesus was growing up nicely.
He always listened to his parents.

One day Mary, Joseph and Jesus travelled to Jerusalem. They went to a festival with all the other Jews to praise God for his greatness.

After the festival Joseph and Mary were on their way home when they made a terrible discovery:
Jesus was missing!

They looked everywhere for him, but Jesus was not with the other children who were part of the group of travellers. Mary and Joseph were so worried. They hurried back to Jerusalem to look for Jesus.
They searched all over the big city ...

At last they found Jesus. He was in the temple. They were so happy to find him. He was busy talking to the clever men about God. The clever men were amazed to hear how much Jesus knew about God.

Back home in Nazareth the people knew that God loved Jesus, and they also loved Jesus very much.

Come, let's pray together:

Jesus, I want to be
just like you.
Amen.

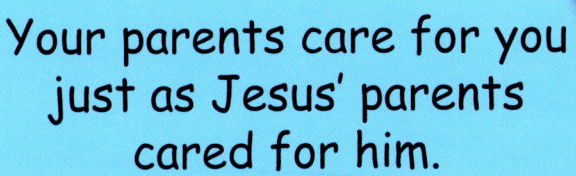

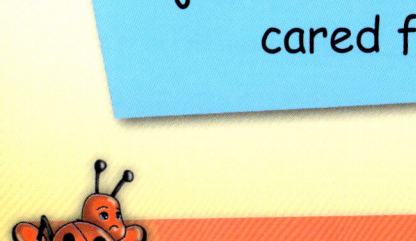

Your parents care for you just as Jesus' parents cared for him.

Do you know the names of Jesus' dad and mom?

16. Five loaves and two fish
(John 6)

Many, many people wanted to hear Jesus talking about God. One day they listened to him until supper time, and the people were very hungry. They had forgotten to bring food with them.

Jesus told his friends to give the people food. Andrew, one of his friends, brought a small boy to Jesus. "This little boy has two fish and five loaves," he said. "But it's not nearly enough to feed this whole crowd of people."

Jesus smiled at the little boy and took the food from him. First, Jesus thanked his Father for the food. Then he shared it out among all the hungry people. And there was enough for everyone! It was a miracle. There was even food left over. Jesus' disciples collected twelve baskets of leftovers.

Come, let's pray together:

Lord Jesus, I know that you can do anything.
Amen.

Jesus performed miracles that no person can ever do.

Can you count the loaves and fishes?

17. There is no one like Jesus
(Luke 8)

One day when Jesus was teaching a crowd of people about God, Jairus pushed his way to the front and fell to his knees. He said to Jesus, "My daughter is very ill. I know you can make her better." Jesus went with Jairus to his house. On the way there, people came running to meet them and told them that the little girl was already dead.

Jesus comforted Jairus. "Don't worry, just believe," he said.

When they reached Jairus' house Jesus told the people to stop crying. He told them the little girl was just asleep, but they laughed at him. Jesus went into the house. He took the little girl's hand and said, "Get up!"

Straight away she was better. Jesus told the family to give her something to eat. Everyone who saw her knew that there is no one like Jesus.

Come, let's pray together:

Lord Jesus, you really are wonderful. I love you very much. Amen.

There is no one like Jesus. Remember, Jesus can really help you.

Whose daughter did Jesus heal?

18. A father opens his arms
(Luke 15)

Jesus loved to tell stories. Here is one of his best ...

Once there was a good father, who loved his two sons very much.

One day the younger boy decided that he wanted to take his money and leave home.

The younger son travelled to a faraway country, where he wasted all his money When the money was all gone, he found a job looking after pigs. He was so hungry that he wanted to eat some of the pig's food.

Things became so tough for him that he decided to go home to his father. His father was hoping he would return. When he saw his son coming down the road, he ran to him and hugged him tight. His father was so happy to see him again that he gave him new clothes and organised a big party to celebrate him coming home.

Come, let's pray together:

Jesus, thank you that you told such wonderful stories, so we could learn how much you love us. Amen.

Our Heavenly Father always loves us.

What did Jesus love to do?

19. The ten girls
(Matthew 25)

Jesus told this story too ...

Ten girls with oil lamps were waiting for a special visitor to arrive. They did not know when the visitor would be there. They kept their lamps burning the whole time, because it was dark.

Sadly, only five of the girls had been clever enough to bring extra oil with them. Before long, all ten girls began to yawn and fall asleep.

Suddenly someone shouted, "Here he is, the important visitor is here!" Quickly the five clever girls filled their lamps with extra oil and lit them.

81

The other five girls had to run to the nearest shop to buy more oil.

The important visitor was very happy to see the five clever girls and they had a lovely party. There were delicious things to eat and to drink.

When the other five girls arrived, it was too late to join the party. They missed all the fun.

Come, let's pray together:

Jesus, I want to bring you joy and have a joyful time with you in heaven one day. Amen.

Always do your best for Jesus, because he always does his best for you.

How many girls had lamps?

20. Bad Zacchaeus becomes Good Zacchaeus (Luke 19)

Zacchaeus was a very rich man who lived in Jericho. Nobody liked him because he was nasty to other people. Zacchaeus. He wanted to see Jesus very badly, but he was too short to see over the heads of the people in the crowd.

The people pushed him out of the way because nobody wanted to stand near the nasty Zacchaeus. So Zacchaeus climbed into a nearby tree. From there he could see Jesus clearly. Jesus saw him straight away.

The people were all astonished when Jesus began to talk to Zacchaeus. And Zacchaeus was amazed when Jesus came to his house to eat a meal with him. From that day onwards "Bad Zacchaeus" became "Good Zacchaeus", and he was always ready to help everyone.

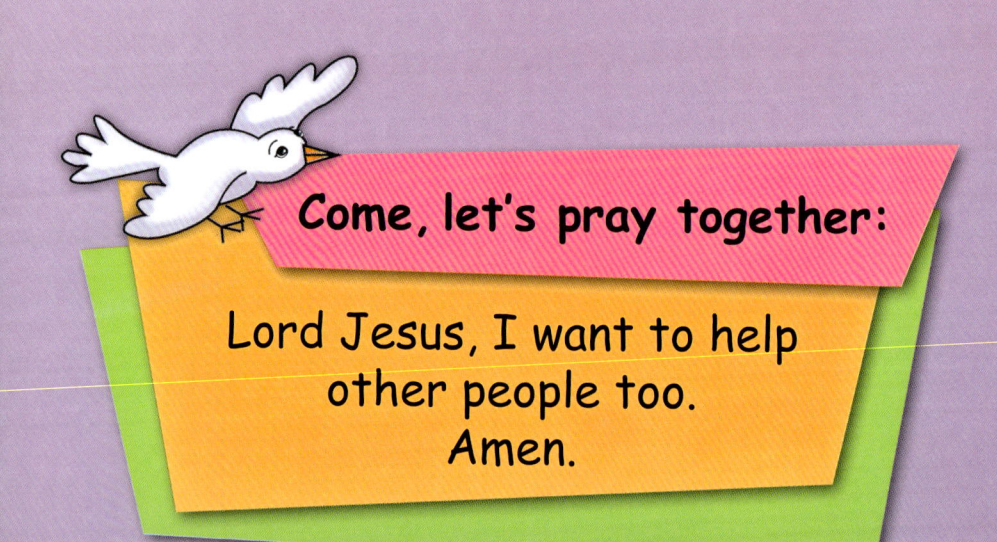

Come, let's pray together:

Lord Jesus, I want to help other people too.
Amen.

People who love Jesus enjoy helping other people.

Name the man who climbed the tree?

21. Here comes King Jesus
(Matthew 21)

When they came near to Jerusalem, Jesus said to his friends, "Bring me a young donkey." He told them where to find the donkey and what they had to say to its owner. Jesus' friends went to the place where the donkey was. They were about to take the donkey when the owner asked, "Why are you taking my donkey?"

"Jesus needs him," they replied. When the man heard this, he was satisfied. He gave the donkey to them straight away.

89

Jesus rode the donkey into the city of Jerusalem. Crowds of people lined the street. They waved palm branches in the air and shouted, "Praise the Lord. Here comes the King!"

Come, let's pray together:

Lord Jesus, I want to sing your praises everyday.
Amen.

Tell everyone that Jesus is king of your life.

Name the animal Jesus rode on?

22. Jesus loves his friends
(John 13)

Jesus and his friends were sitting around the dinner table. Jesus saw that his friends' feet were dirty, because they had been walking in the streets all day in their sandals.

He took off his robe and tied a towel around his waist. Then he poured water into a basin. He began to wash his friends' feet, drying them with a towel afterwards. Peter was one of Jesus' best friends. Naturally he did not want Jesus as his leader, to wash his feet. "You will never wash my feet," he said.

93

Jesus answered, "If I don't wash your feet, you will not be part of me." So Peter allowed Jesus to wash his feet.

Jesus did this to show his friends how much he loved and cared for them.

Come, let's pray together:

Jesus, help me to always
love my friends.
Amen.

Remember to do special things for your friends.

What did Jesus do for His friends?

95

23. The cross
(Matthew 27)

Jesus' enemies wanted to kill him. They went to Pontius Pilate, the most important man in the country.
They told him to find Jesus guilty of a crime; but Pilate could not find anything that Jesus had done wrong.

Pilate decided to ask the people what he should do. When they saw Jesus they all shouted, "Crucify him!"
Jesus' enemies had told them to do this. Pilate told them to crucify Jesus at a place called Golgotha. There they hung Jesus on a cross between two criminals.

97

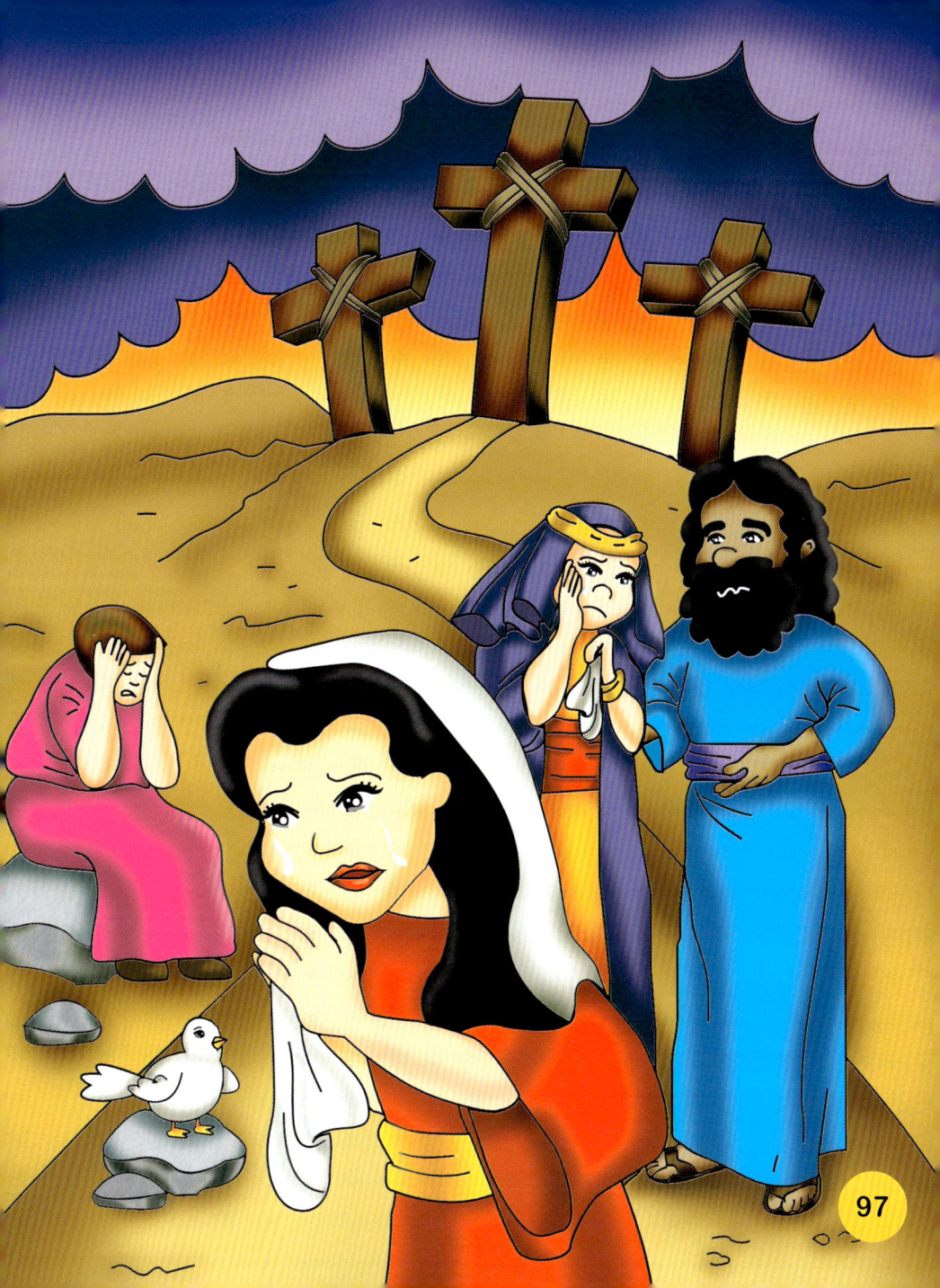

While he was dying on the cross, Jesus asked God to forgive those same people who were being so cruel to him.

Jesus died on a Friday afternoon which is now known as Good Friday, because on that day Jesus made it possible for people to be friends with God once again.

Come, let's pray together:

Lord Jesus, thank you that you died on the cross for my sins.
Amen.

Jesus died on the cross so that all the wrong things we do — our sins — can be forgiven.

Name the place Jesus was crucified?

24. Jesus has risen from the dead! (Matthew 28)

Jesus was buried that Friday in a cave that belonged to his friend Joseph. Everyone was very sad.

Early on the Sunday morning a group of women went to the grave.
They wondered how they would get inside the cave, because a big stone had already been rolled in front of the entrance. But when they got there they found that the stone had already been rolled away . . . and that the grave was empty!

An angel told them that Jesus had risen from the dead.

101

They were so happy. They rushed back to tell the rest of Jesus' friends the good news. One of the women, Mary Magdalene, went back to the empty grave. "Mary!" she heard someone calling her name. Right away she knew it was Jesus. She ran to tell the others that she had seen Jesus with her own eyes.

Come, let's pray together:

Lord Jesus, thank you that you are alive, and that I will live with you forever. Amen.

Jesus is alive!
And everyone who loves him will live with him forever, even when they die.

Who saw Jesus with her own eyes?

25. Jesus returns home
(Acts 1)

Jesus' friends were so happy to have him back. They knew that nobody is as powerful as he is. He is even stronger than death.

One day Jesus told them that he had to go back to be with his father in heaven, because heaven is his true home. He also told them not to be sad, because one day they would all join him there!

Jesus and his friends then climbed to the top of a mountain.

105

A cloud came down and covered them. When the cloud lifted, it took Jesus away. Jesus' friends watched him going to heaven with sad hearts.

Suddenly they saw two angels standing there. The angels said to the disciples (this is the name given to Jesus' special friends) that Jesus would come back one day. They had to go and tell the whole world that Jesus loves everybody.

Come, let's pray together:

Lord Jesus, I know you will return to take me to heaven, because the Bible tells me so. Amen.

Even though Jesus is in heaven, we know he still takes care of us.

Where did the cloud take Jesus?

Guidelines for parents

Temperament Icon
Every child is unique – yet there are certain characteristics shared by all human beings which can be divided into four temperaments. Some children thrive in a situation where there are definite rules, a steady routine and responsibilities (routine children); others prefer living in the moment and enjoy doing things (action children); then there are those who like to solve problems creatively, even if it means doing it differently than the known way (why children) and lastly we have children who live according to their vivid imaginations and values (the imaginative, people-orientated children). CMP books are developed so that they will appeal to and stimulate each temperament type. For more information regarding the temperaments visit the CMP website www.cmpublishing.co.za

Development Icon
CMP books take into account the different developmental phases of children. Our aim is to assist parents and caregivers to intellectually and emotionally stimulate children to ensure maximum growth in these areas. For more information visit the CMP website www.cmpublishing.co.za

Faith Icon
The formation of faith is indeed unique to each child; there are however general characteristics which apply to all children. There are three main ways that children develop faith:
- Parents regularly reading the Bible, telling Bible and other faith based stories, praying together and doing faith building activities with their children (such as the ones found in this book).
- Children ask questions – parents need to take these questions seriously and answer them according to the child's level of understanding.
- Children follow the example of those caring for them.

Emotional intelligence icon
We experience emotions long before we learn the language to be able to express how we are feeling. Therefore it is important that children are taught to verbalise what they are feeling. Use the illustrations accompanying the stories and ask your child how they think the people or animals in the picture feel. This helps them become aware of their own emotions as well as those of others. It provides a learning opportunity where the child can learn appropriate words to express how they are feeling.

Reading icon
A wonderful world opens up for your child when they start learning to read. Enjoy every moment of this exciting adventure with your child. Let them sit on your lap where they can be comfortable and feel safe and secure. Open the book holding it so that you can both see the pages. Read clearly and with enthusiasm. As you know you can read the same story over and over. Point out where you are reading with your finger as you go along. This will help your child to begin to see the relationship between letters, sounds, words and their meaning. Encourage your child's attempts at reading – even of it sounds like gibberish.

Listening skills icon
Listening is an important learning and development skill. You can help develop this skill in your child by encouraging them to listen attentively, and understand what they are hearing. Let them look at the illustrations and then use their imagination to tell the story back to you in their own words. You can also encourage them to do this by asking questions relating to the story. Yet another way is to leave out words from a story the child knows well and let them fill in the missing words.

Vocabulary icon
Use every opportunity to build your child's vocabulary – it is a lifelong gift which you are giving to them. Start with everyday objects and people in the illustrations in books. Point at the picture, say the word, form a short sentence using the word. Repeat it again and then let your child say the word. Try to use the word in another context – if there is a tent in the picture you are looking at then say: we sleep in a tent when we go camping.

Speech formation icon
Right from the word go build your child's vocabulary – words are the building blocks of speech. Continually name objects around you, pointing them out, make sure your child looks at your mouth, feeling your lips and throat as you pronounce the words. As your child grows, gently increase the difficulty of the words used stretching your child's understanding. Strongly encourage your child's first attempts at speaking. Help your child to pronounce the sounds and words. At this stage accuracy is not as important as trying.

Numeracy skills icon
It is important for your child develop numeracy skills. Play simple games such as: "How many ducks are there in the picture? If we add two more ducks how many are there now? Then if three fly away? (use your fingers to illustrate this) How many are left? They also need to recognise the shape of numbers – cut large numbers from cardboard – let your child play with these – place the numbers in order forming a line from one to ten.

The YesKids Bible
Stories & Prayers

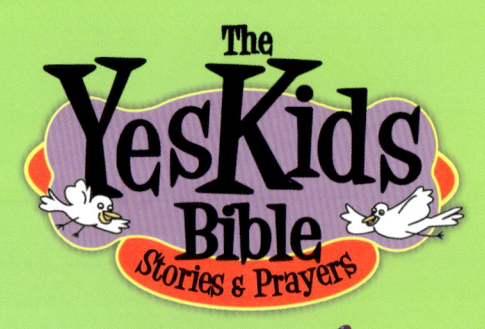

cmp
christian media publishing Kids
pointing children in the **right direction**

© All rights reserved

Christian Media Publishers,
PO Box 4502, Durbanville, 7551
www.christianmediapublishing.com

Author: Ewald van Rensburg

Illustrations, Design & Layout: Lilani Brits

Publishing Project Manager: Noeline N Neumann

Reg No 2010/008573/07

No part of this publication may be reproduced by any means – electronically or otherwise – without the prior written permission of the publisher.

Text: Maranatha Publishing: Used by kind agreement.

Printed and bound in China.
First edition, first printing 2012

ISBN 978-1-920593-28-5